Birthday Cakes
For Kids

CRESCENT BOOKS

This edition published by:
Crescent Books
Distributed by Outlet Book Company, Inc.
A Random House Company
40 Englehard Ave.
Avenel, New Jersey 07001

Printed in U.S.A.

ISBN 0-517-06089-2

Photography on pages 12, 50, 70, 74 and 88 by Sanders Studios, Inc.
Food Stylist: Mary Helen Steindler

Remaining photography and food styling: Burke/Triolo Studio.

Diagrams drawn by Rowena Jatico

Pictured on the front cover (*clockwise from bottom*): Teddy Bear Train (*page 78*), Flying Kites
(*page 28*) and Rex the Dinosaur (*page 60*).

Pictured on the back cover (*clockwise from bottom left*): Tic-Tac-Toe (*page 82*), Touchdown
Football (*page 84*) and Dream Castle (*page 26*).

CONTENTS

BEFORE YOU BEGIN

What could be a happier occasion than a child's birthday party? You can make your child's party even more special with a unique birthday cake decorated by you! Each of the fabulous cakes in BIRTHDAY CAKES FOR KIDS is beautifully photographed and has easy-to-follow step-by-step directions.

The cakes are marked with one, two or three birthday candles to signify the time and skill needed. If you are a beginner, you may want to start with cakes marked with one candle. Then, as your confidence builds, move on to cakes with two or three candles. **Read through the following information before starting.** You will discover many helpful tips and important guidelines to make your cake decorating easier and more fun!

SPECIAL EQUIPMENT

The right equipment not only makes cake decorating easier but also gives more professional

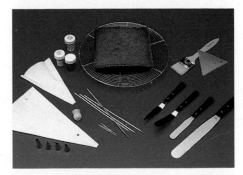

Special Equipment (*clockwise from bottom left*): Assorted decorating tips, pastry bags, coupler, wooden picks and skewers, paste colors, cooling rack, pastry brush, cake comb and assorted spatulas.

results. All of the equipment mentioned here is available in stores carrying cake decorating supplies.

Flexible metal spatulas of various sizes are useful in applying frosting. Use one with a narrow tip to get into small areas. A large flexible metal spatula makes smoothing the frosting on large flat areas easier.

Wooden picks and wooden or metal skewers are useful for marking designs and lines on the cakes.

Paste food colors are recommended for coloring the frosting as they do not thin the frosting like liquid colorings and they create bright, vibrant colors. For more information on coloring frosting see page 9.

A **pastry bag** with several tips is essential for piping decorations. The pastry bag can be a reusable bag, a plastic disposable bag or a bag folded from a parchment paper triangle. We recommend the following basic **decorating tips:** several sizes of writing tips (*numbers 3, 5, 9 and 12*), a star tip (*number 28*) and a basketweave tip (*number 47*). See page 11 for a photo and in-depth explanation of various decorating tips.

A **coupler** inserted into the pastry bag before filling makes changing tips easier. See page 10 for additional information on the coupler and how it is used.

An **icing comb** can be used to create lines and patterns in frosting (see page 58).

Cake boards are made of heavy cardboard and are used for cakes that are too large to fit on a plate or tray. See page 8 for instructions on how to cover cake boards.

BASIC CAKE KNOW-HOW

Cake Mixes vs. Cakes from Scratch

Using a packaged cake mix can save time, but be aware that cakes made from mixes are usually more tender and crumbly than cakes made from scratch. Place the cooled cake in the freezer for 30 to 45 minutes to firm cake for easier cutting, frosting and decorating. If the birthday cake you choose has many small pieces that may be difficult to cut and frost, use one of the cake recipes on pages 92 and 93, or your own favorite recipe. Be sure to use a layer of Base Frosting (see page 94) to seal in the crumbs.

The Best Baking Pans

For great cakes, use shiny metal pans or pans with a nonstick finish. Grease and flour all pans before adding the cake batter. *Even nonstick pans should be lightly greased.* To grease a pan, spread a thin layer of vegetable shortening on the bottom and sides of the cake pan. Add a small amount of flour then tilt and shake the pan until flour covers the bottom and sides. Shake out any excess flour. *Or*, grease and line pan bottom with waxed paper (flouring the pan is unnecessary). See tip on this page about removing waxed paper liners.

Dividing the Batter

When baking layer cakes, it is important to divide the batter equally between the pans to make even layers. Either measure the batter and divide it equally (for example, 2 cups of batter in each pan) or weigh the pans after adding the batter. With practice, you will be able to judge by eye whether the batter in each pan is equal. Spread the batter evenly in the pans before baking.

Testing for Doneness

Always bake cakes at the oven temperature and time specified in the recipe. Test cakes after the shortest time given. A cake is done when a wooden pick inserted into the center comes out clean. It should pull away from the side of the pan and spring back when lightly touched in the center. White and yellow cakes should be lightly browned.

Cooling Cakes

Let cakes cool in the pan on a wire rack for about 10 minutes. Loosen cake edges with a spatula, place the rack, top-side down, over the pan. Flip the rack and the pan over together and the cake should drop out onto the rack. If it does not come out, tap the bottom of the pan; the cake should come out easily. Remove the pan. If using a waxed paper liner, carefully peel it off while the cake is still warm. Place a second wire rack over the cake and flip both racks and the cake back over so the cake can cool, top-side up. Remove the top rack. If a cake is removed from the pan too soon, it may crack and break. If it is allowed to cool too long, it may stick to the pan. Always cool a cake completely before frosting.

Storing Cakes

Cool cakes completely before covering and storing. If using the undecorated layers within two days, wrap tightly in foil or plastic wrap and store in a cool place. For longer storage, wrap in heavy-duty foil or place in airtight freezer bags; freeze for up to two months. To thaw, remove the layers from the freezer and let them thaw, wrapped, at room temperature.

For storing decorated cakes, first set frosting and decorations by freezing unwrapped cake for 1 to 2 hours or until the frosting has hardened. Wrap tightly and freeze up to one month. Unwrap before thawing.

BEFORE FROSTING

Trimming Cakes

Trimmed cakes are easier to frost and give more professional results. For best results, use a serrated knife long enough to cut across the top of the cake in one stroke. Use a gentle sawing motion as you cut through the cake. The rounded tops of round, square and rectangular cakes should be trimmed to form a flat surface.

The sides of cakes that are square or rectangular should also be trimmed to make them more even.

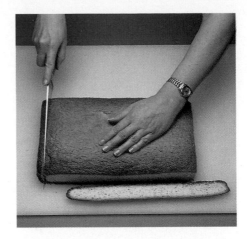

Use a soft pastry brush to remove all loose cake crumbs. Brush away crumbs again after cutting cake.

Cutting cakes

For cleaner cutting lines and fewer crumbs, freeze the cake for 30 to 45 minutes.

When cutting each cake design, use the diagrams and photos as a guide and follow the directions carefully. A ruler and wooden

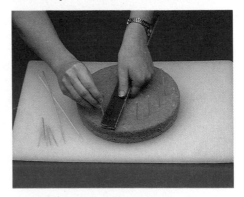

picks are helpful to mark designs and act as a guide while cutting. The shaded areas in the diagrams are unused portions of cake. Carefully position all pieces on a plate, tray or cake board. Connect the pieces with some of the frosting.

Leftover cake scraps can be used in a number of ways. Layer them with pudding or softened ice cream for a wonderful parfait. Serve under fresh berries and fruit as a sweet shortcake or use as the base for a trifle. Or, sprinkle crumbs on top of desserts or sundaes. And, easiest of all, they make a wonderful snack for hungry cooks and kids.

Assembling Cakes

Many decorated cakes are too large for standard plates and platters. Use cake boards, cutting boards, cookie sheets or other large flat surfaces. Cake boards can be covered with foil, greaseproof paper, paper doilies or plastic wrap. To cover, cut the foil or paper 1 to 2 inches larger than the board. Center the board on the reverse side of the paper. Cut slashes in the paper almost to the board along any place that is curved. This allows the paper to fit smoothly over the board. Fold the edges over the board and tape into place. If a cake is very large or heavy, two cake boards may be stacked together before covering for additional support.

To keep the plate or covered board clean, tuck strips of waxed paper underneath the assembled cake before frosting. When decorating is complete, carefully slide out the strips and touch up frosting as needed.

THE FROSTING STORY
Frosting Consistency

The proper frosting consistency is the secret to successful decorating. Buttercream Frosting (page 95) should hold its shape when scooped with a spatula. If

the frosting is too soft because the kitchen is warm, try refrigerating the frosting for about 15 minutes and keep it chilled while you work. If the frosting is soft because liquid coloring was used or too much milk was added, beat in some additional sifted powdered sugar. If the frosting is too stiff to spread easily, beat in additional milk, a small amount at a time, until the desired consistency is achieved.

Canned Frostings

Commercially prepared canned frostings can also be used for cake decorating. Color and use for piping just like buttercream frosting. For best results, refrigerate the frosting first and keep chilled while decorating. One (16-ounce) can of frosting equals about 1½ cups.

Base Frosting

Frosting cakes with Base Frosting (page 94) is a professional technique that is simple to do, gives the cake a smoother, cleaner finish and makes frosting the cake much easier. Spread a thin layer of base frosting, or frosting thinned with milk, on all sides of the cake after cutting and positioning the pieces. This base coat helps to seal in the crumbs, preventing them from showing up in the final layer of buttercream frosting. Let the base frosting dry a few minutes before covering with buttercream frosting.

A glaze can be used instead of base frosting to add moistness, flavor and to seal in the crumbs. Brush the Jam Glaze (page 94) over the cut cake and allow it to set before frosting. Use a light-colored glaze for a cake with a white or light-colored frosting. A berry glaze is particularly good with a chocolate cake and chocolate frosting.

Coloring Frosting

We recommend you use paste colors (available at stores carrying cake decorating supplies) because they do not thin the frosting. If liquid food coloring is used, you may have to add more powdered sugar to get the frosting back to the desired consistency. When cocoa powder is added for flavor and color, some milk may need to be added.

To tint frosting with paste colors, add a small amount of the paste color with a wooden pick and stir well. Slowly add more color until the frosting is the desired shade. With liquid food colors, add the coloring drop by drop, mixing well after each drop, until the desired shade is reached. Paste colors are available in a wide variety of colors, but you can also make almost any color by mixing the basics: red, green, yellow, blue and black.

The following chart shows how these basic colors can be mixed to produce many frosting colors called for in this book. The numbers refer to the ratio of one color to another (i.e. orange is made by mixing 1 part red food coloring with 3 parts yellow food coloring). These ratios can be used for both paste and liquid food colorings.

To Make:	Red	Green	Yellow	Blue		Black
Rose	5			1	OR	1
Orange	1		3			
Peach	1		2			
Olive Green		2	1			1
Medium Blue				1		1
Purple	1			1		
Brown	2	2	1			

Storing Frosting

Buttercream frosting can be made ahead of time. Refrigerate it in an airtight container and use within two days. Or freeze it for up to one month. When ready to use, bring frosting to room temperature; beat well with electric mixer.

DECORATING TECHNIQUES

Frosting Cakes

To frost a cake, place a mound of frosting in the center of the cake. Spread frosting across the top by pushing it out toward the sides with a spatula. Always keep the spatula on a frosted surface, because once it touches the cake surface, crumbs will mix in with the frosting. To frost the sides, work from the top down, making sure the spatula only touches frosting.

Using a Pastry Bag

A coupler can save time and mess but it is not necessary for successful cake decorating. It is used to attach tips to the pastry bag and allows you to change tips without removing the frosting from the bag. To use, unscrew the ring,

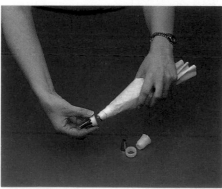

insert the cone-shaped piece into the narrow end of the pastry bag until the end extends slightly beyond the end of the bag (snip off the end of the pastry bag if necessary), then place the decorating tip on the end. Screw the ring on to hold the tip in place.

To change tips, unscrew the ring, remove the tip, place the new tip on and screw the ring back in place.

To fill a pastry bag with frosting, insert the decorating tip or attach the tip with a coupler. Fold the top of the bag down as shown, then use a spatula to place the frosting in the bag. Fill the bag only about half full, then unfold top of the bag. Twist the top of the bag down tightly against the frosting.

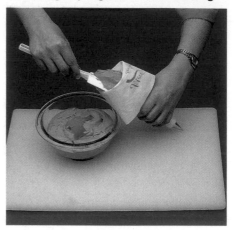

Grip the pastry bag near the top with the twisted end between thumb and forefinger. Place the other hand near the tip as shown. Using even pressure, squeeze the frosting out while guiding the tip. Do not loosen your grip on the twisted end or the frosting will begin to push up and out of the top of the bag.

Piped Decorations

Different decorating tips produce different piped decorations. Writing tips have round holes, and make smooth lines perfect for lettering and outlining. The basketweave tip can be used in two ways. The smooth side makes a wide flat ribbon of frosting. The ridged side makes a wide ridged frosting stripe. A star

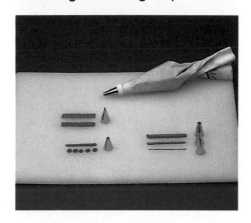

tip makes individual stars or fancy ridged stripes and zigzags. With a little practice, there is no end to the variety of piped decorations you can make.

SERVING

Before serving cakes, remove any inedible decorations or wooden picks.

Portion size

The suggested number of servings for each cake is based on child-size portions served with ice cream. If several adults are included, the cake will serve fewer people.

HAVE FUN

Feel free to use your own colors and candies when decorating the cakes. Don't lock yourself in to the suggested decorations in the photos. You may want to match the cake to the party favors or use a child's favorite candies to decorate a cake. Try using one of the cake designs as the centerpiece for a birthday party and continue the theme of the cake with invitations, tablecloth, napkins and other decorations. Party games and take-home favors can also be coordinated to complete the theme. The important thing is to have fun and let your imagination and creativity take over.

TIPS FOR A SUCCESSFUL KID'S BIRTHDAY PARTY

Number of Guests

To determine the number of children to invite, take the age of the child, add one and invite that many guests. For example, a birthday party for a 5-year-old child might have a guest list of six children.

Games and Activities

Most parties need not be longer than 2 hours to open presents, play games and have cake and ice cream. Keep the age of the children in mind when planning the games. They should challenge but not be too difficult to understand. A mixture of familiar games and a few new ones should keep the children busy and entertained. In order to keep everyone happy and avoid hurt feelings, try to plan non-competitive games or find alternative ways to play. Creative activities can be fun and they give each child a special gift to take home when the party is over. Whatever the activity—creating hats or masks, designing T-shirts or ornaments—start with something basic and let the children add decorations. Remember to protect the children's clothes and your furniture.

ALPHABET BLOCK

CAKES & FROSTINGS

4 (8-inch) square cakes
7 cups Buttercream Frosting (page 95)*
1½ cups Base Frosting (page 94), if desired

DECORATIONS & EQUIPMENT

Pastel candy-coated chocolate mints
Chocolate sprinkles
Pink colored sugar
2 (19×13-inch) cake boards**
Ice cream cone-shaped cookie cutter
Pastry bag and medium writing tip

1. Trim tops and edges of cakes to make tops level and all cakes of equal size.

2. Place 1 cake layer on covered cake board. Frost top with ¾ cup white frosting. Place second cake layer on frosting. Frost top with ¾ cup white frosting.

3. Place remaining cake board on top of cake. Top with third cake layer. Frost top with ¾ cup white frosting. Place fourth cake layer on top.

4. Frost entire cake with Base Frosting to seal in crumbs.

5. Frost opposite sides of cake with blue frosting. Frost remaining 2 sides with green frosting. Frost top of cake with 1 cup white frosting.

6. Outline edges with chocolate mints as shown in photo.

7. Using cookie cutter, make outline on top of block. Using writing tip and remaining white frosting, pipe outline of design. Fill with sprinkles and colored sugar, as shown.

8. Slice and serve top 2 layers of cake first. To serve bottom section, remove cake board and slice into pieces.
Makes 32 to 36 servings

*Color 1½ cups frosting pastel blue and 1½ cups pastel green; reserve 4 cups white frosting.

**Cut boards into two 7×7-inch squares; stack and cover. Cut 6½×6½-inch square from remaining piece.

Use your creativity to personalize the cake you are decorating. Feel free to add favorite colors and candies. For the Alphabet Block, it might be fun to spell out the child's name or initials in candy or depict a special toy on the top of the cake.

BIRTHDAY WATCH

CAKES & FROSTINGS

1 (8-inch) square cake
1 (9-inch) round cake
3½ cups Buttercream Frosting
    (page 95)*
1 cup Base Frosting
    (page 94), if desired

DECORATIONS & EQUIPMENT

Pink colored sugar
Assorted candies
1 (19×13-inch) cake board,
    cut to fit cake, if
    desired, and covered
Pastry bag and medium
    writing tip

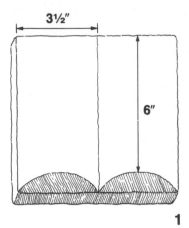

1

1. Trim tops and edges of cakes. Cut square cake as shown in diagram 1.

2. Position cakes on prepared cake board as shown in diagram 2, connecting with some of the medium pink frosting. Trim opposite ends to fit on cake board, if needed.

3. Frost entire cake with Base Frosting to seal in crumbs.

4. Frost top of round cake with light pink frosting, leaving 1-inch rim around edge. Frost sides and rim with blue frosting, reserving ½ cup portion for piping. Sprinkle blue area with colored sugar.

5. Frost band with medium pink frosting. Using writing tip and reserved blue frosting, pipe numbers on face and swirls on band as shown in photo. Arrange assorted candies on watch face.
Makes 16 to 20 servings

*Color 1½ cups frosting medium pink, 1 cup light pink and 1 cup blue.

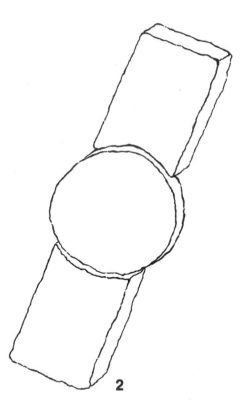

2

BOO THE GHOST

CAKE & FROSTING
- 1 (13×9-inch) cake
- 2 cups Light & Fluffy Frosting (page 95)

DECORATIONS & EQUIPMENT
- 2 black licorice drops or jelly beans
- Plastic spiders, if desired
- 1 (19×13-inch) cake board, cut in half crosswise and covered

1. Trim top and edges of cake. Using diagram as guide, draw ghost pattern on 13×9-inch piece of waxed paper. Cut pattern out and place on cake. Cut out ghost. Place on prepared cake board.

2. Frost ghost, swirling frosting.

3. Arrange licorice drops for eyes and spiders as shown in photo.

Makes 12 to 14 servings

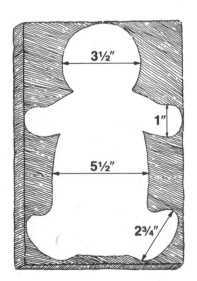

CATCH-U-LATER CALCULATOR

CAKE & FROSTINGS

    1 (13×9-inch) cake
    3 cups Buttercream Frosting
       (page 95)*
    1 cup Base Frosting
       (page 94), if desired

DECORATIONS & EQUIPMENT

    6 green candy discs
  10 pink candy discs
    1 (19×13-inch) cake board,
      cut in half crosswise
      and covered
     Pastry bag, medium and
     large writing tips

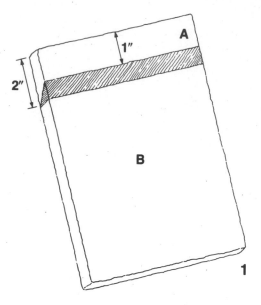

1. Trim top and edges of cake. Cut as shown in diagram 1.

2. Place piece B on prepared cake board. Attach piece A with some of the pink frosting, placing angled side toward opposite end of cake for calculator display area as shown in diagram 2.

3. Frost entire cake with Base Frosting to seal in crumbs.

4. Using wooden pick, draw area about 1 inch from edges of cake. Frost area with white frosting, as shown in photo.

5. Frost remaining cake with pink frosting.

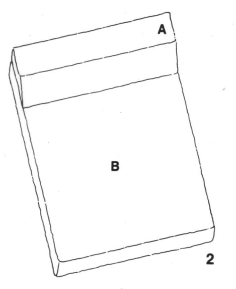

6. Arrange candy discs as shown. Using medium writing tip and brown frosting, pipe numbers 0 through 9 on pink candy discs. Pipe decimal point, plus, minus, times, equal and division symbols on green candy discs.

7. Pipe a line around white area and pipe child's age in the display area. Using large writing tip, pipe border around display area.

Makes 16 to 20 servings

*Color 1½ cups frosting pink and ½ cup dark brown; reserve 1 cup white frosting.

18

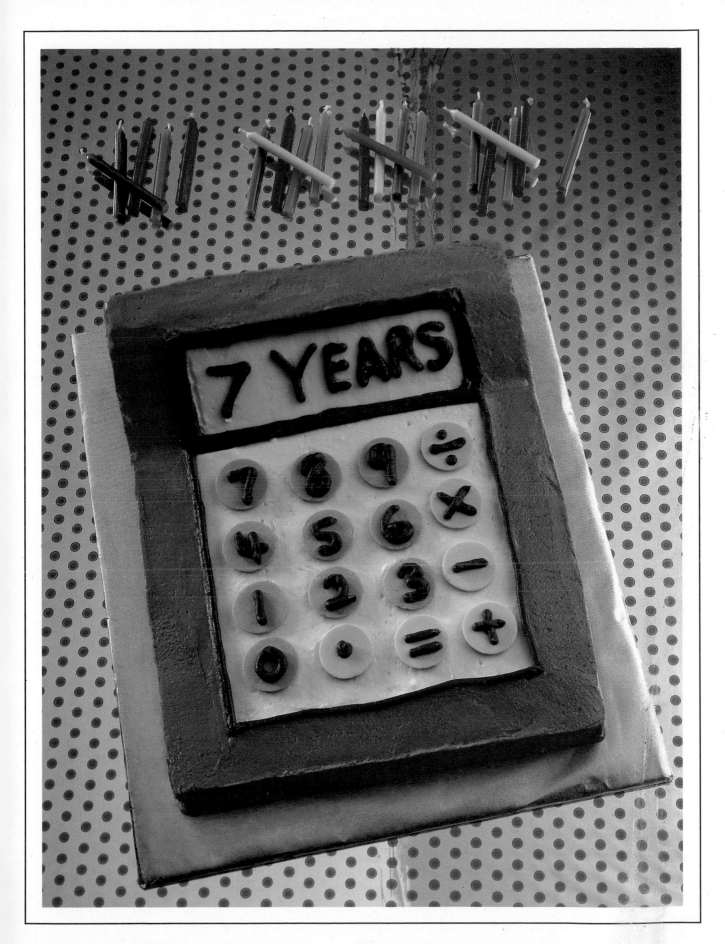

19

COCOA THE CAT

CAKES & FROSTINGS

- 1 (13×9-inch) cake
- 1 (9-inch) round cake
- 2¾ cups Buttercream Frosting (page 95)*
- 1½ cups Base Frosting (page 94), if desired

DECORATIONS & EQUIPMENT

- 1 cup flaked coconut, tinted brown**
- 2½ cups flaked coconut, tinted tan**
- 2 blue candies or gumballs
- 1 black licorice whip
- 1 small red gumdrop
- Assorted candies
- 1 (19×13-inch) cake board, cut to fit cake, if desired, and covered
- Pastry bag and large writing tip

1. Trim tops and edges of cakes. Using diagram 1 as guide, draw cat body, ears and tail on 13×9-inch piece of waxed paper. Cut pattern out and place on cake. Cut out pieces. Cut one edge of round cake to form flat edge.

2. Position pieces on prepared cake board as shown in diagram 2, connecting with some of the cocoa frosting.

3. Frost entire cake with Base Frosting to seal in crumbs.

4. Frost again with cocoa frosting.

5. Using wooden pick, outline area for feet, tip of tail, edges of ears and face as shown in photo. Sprinkle with brown coconut.

6. Sprinkle remaining areas with tan coconut.

7. Using writing tip and blue frosting, pipe ovals for eyes; add blue candies.

8. Arrange short pieces of licorice whip for whiskers. Cut a slice off bottom of red gumdrop for nose. Arrange assorted candies for collar.

Makes 18 to 22 servings

Mix 2½ cups frosting with 2 tablespoons unsweetened cocoa powder. Color ¼ cup frosting bright blue.

**See tip on tinting coconut, page 42.*

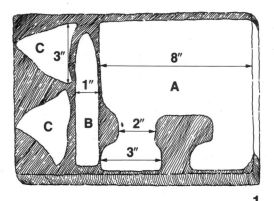

1

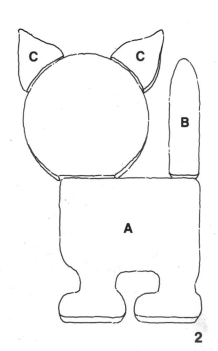

2

CORKY THE CLOWN

CAKES & FROSTINGS

- 1 (9-inch) square cake
- 1 (9-inch) round cake
- 3 cups Buttercream Frosting (page 95)*
- 1½ cups Base Frosting (page 94), If desired

DECORATIONS & EQUIPMENT

- Assorted candies
- 1 (19×13-inch) cake board, cut to fit cake, if desired, and covered
- Pastry bags, medium writing tip and star tip

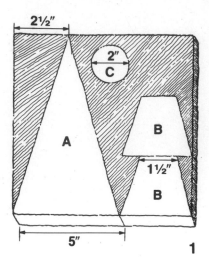

1

1. Trim tops and edges of cakes. Cut square cake as shown in diagram 1.

2. Position pieces on prepared cake board as shown in diagram 2, connecting with some of the white frosting.

3. Frost entire cake with Base Frosting to seal in crumbs.

4. Frost face with white frosting. Using writing tip and pink frosting, pipe mouth.

5. Frost bow tie and top of hat with yellow frosting as shown in photo. Frost hat with some of the orange frosting. Using star tip and orange frosting, pipe design on hat and bow tie.

6. Arrange assorted candies as shown.

Makes 16 to 18 servings

Color ¾ cup frosting orange, ½ cup yellow and ¼ cup pink; reserve 1½ cups white frosting.

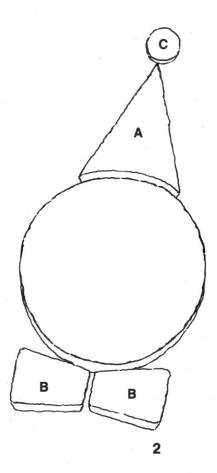

2

DANCING FLOWER II

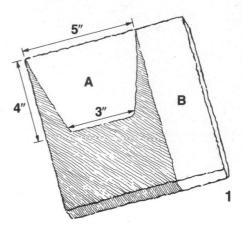

CAKES & FROSTINGS

- 1 (8-inch) square cake
- 1 (9-inch) round cake
- 3 cups Buttercream Frosting (page 95)*
- 1½ cups Base Frosting (page 94), if desired

DECORATIONS & EQUIPMENT

- Thin chocolate wafer cookies
- Chocolate chips
- Assorted candies
- Spearmint candy leaves
- 1 (19×13-inch) cake board, covered
- Pastry bag and small writing tip

1. Trim tops and edges of cakes. Cut square cake as shown in diagram 1.

2. Position pieces on prepared cake board as shown in diagram 2, connecting with some of the pink frosting.

3. Frost entire cake with Base Frosting to seal in crumbs.

4. Frost as shown in photo. Arrange chocolate cookies around outer edge of round cake. Outline inside edge of circle with chocolate chips.

5. Using writing tip and blue frosting, pipe sunglasses as shown. Arrange candies for cheeks and mouth.

6. Add green leaves to stem; attach with frosting, if needed.
   Makes 14 to 18 servings

Color 1½ cups frosting pink, ¾ cup yellow, ½ cup green and ¼ cup blue.

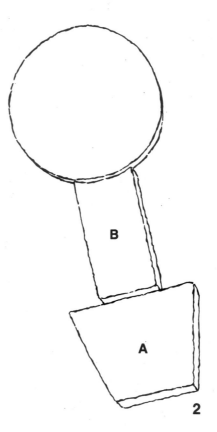

DREAM CASTLE

CAKES & FROSTINGS

  3 (8-inch) square cakes
5¼ cups Buttercream Frosting
  (page 95)*
  2 cups Base Frosting
  (page 94), if desired

DECORATIONS & EQUIPMENT

  Assorted colored sugar
4 sugar ice cream cones
  Small purple and white
  gumdrops
  Pastel candy-coated
  chocolate pieces
2 pink sugar wafer cookies
1 (19×13-inch) cake board,
  cut in half crosswise
  and covered

1. Trim tops and edges of cakes. Place one square cake on prepared cake board. Frost top with some of the white frosting.

2. Cut remaining cakes as shown in diagrams 1 and 2.

3. Place piece A over bottom layer. Frost top of piece A with some of the white frosting.

4. Position remaining pieces as shown in diagram 3, connecting with some of the white frosting.

5. Frost entire cake with Base Frosting to seal in crumbs.

6. Frost again with white frosting. Cover piece D (bridge) with colored sugar.

7. Frost cones with blue and yellow frostings (see Tip). Place as shown in photo.

8. Decorate castle and towers as shown, using frosting to attach candies, if needed.

9. Arrange wafer cookies on front of castle for gate.
    Makes 24 to 28 servings

*Color ½ cup frosting blue and ½ cup yellow; reserve 4¼ cups white frosting.

Tip: For easier frosting of cones, hold cone over fingers of one hand while frosting with other hand. Place in position, touching up frosting, if needed.

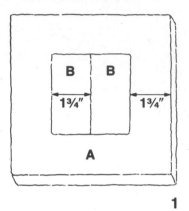

1

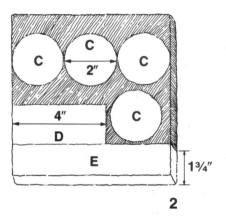

2

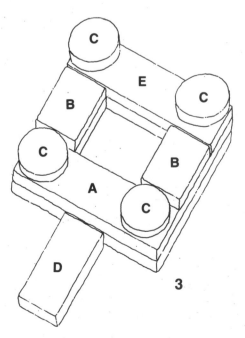

3

FLYING KITES

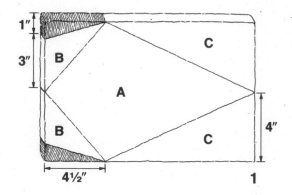

CAKE & FROSTINGS

1 (13×9-inch) cake
3½ cups Buttercream Frosting
    (page 95)*
1½ cups Base Frosting
    (page 94), if desired

DECORATIONS & EQUIPMENT

4 small purple gumdrops
2 small green gumdrops
1 (19×13-inch) cake board,
    covered
    Pastry bags and medium
    writing tip

1. Trim top and edges of cake. Cut as shown in diagram 1.

2. Position pieces on prepared cake board as shown in diagram 2 and photo, connecting with some of the frostings.

3. Frost cakes with Base Frosting to seal in crumbs.

4. Frost again as shown in photo, reserving small portion of each color frosting for piping.

5. Using writing tip, pipe reserved frostings onto kites in contrasting colors. Pipe crosspieces as shown from corner to corner, continuing onto board for tails.

6. Roll out gumdrops and cut each into a triangle.** Arrange triangles on tails of kites as shown.

Makes 16 to 20 servings

Color 1½ cups frosting rose, 1¼ cups light green and ¾ cup medium blue.

**To roll out gumdrops, place, small end up, on a surface lightly sprinkled with sugar. Roll to desired shape and thickness with rolling pin. Flattened gumdrops can be cut in the shape of flowers, leaves and other designs.*

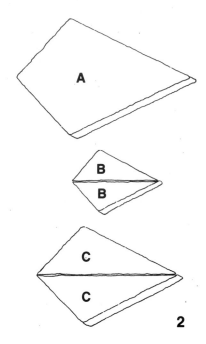

GINGERBREAD MAN

CAKE & FROSTINGS

- 1 (13×9-inch) cake
- 1 recipe Jam Glaze
  (page 94), if desired
- 2 cups Chocolate
  Buttercream Frosting
  (page 95)
- ½ cup Buttercream Frosting
  (page 95)

DECORATIONS & EQUIPMENT

- Assorted candies
- 1 (19×13-inch) cake board,
  cut in half crosswise
  and covered
- Pastry bag and medium
  writing tip

1. Trim top and edges of cake. Using diagram as guide, draw gingerbread man pattern on 13×9-inch piece of waxed paper. Cut pattern out and place on cake. Cut out gingerbread man. Place on prepared cake board.

2. Brush cake lightly with Jam Glaze. Let dry 1 hour.

3. Frost with chocolate frosting.

4. Using writing tip and white frosting, pipe as shown in photo.

5. Arrange assorted candies as shown.

Makes 10 to 14 servings

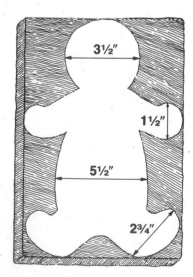

GUMBALL MACHINE

CAKES & FROSTINGS
   1 (9-inch) round cake
   1 (8-inch) square cake
3½ cups Buttercream Frosting
     (page 95)*
   1 cup Base Frosting
     (page 94), if desired

DECORATIONS & EQUIPMENT
   Gumballs
   1 black licorice twist
   Foil-covered chocolate
     coins
   1 red licorice whip
   1 (19×13-inch) cake board,
     cut in half crosswise
     and covered

1. Trim tops and edges of cakes. Cut cake as shown in diagram 1.

2. Position pieces on prepared cake board as shown in diagram 2, connecting with some of the white frosting.

3. Frost entire cake with Base Frosting to seal in crumbs.

4. Using wooden pick, draw coin insertion area as shown in photo. Frost with gray frosting. Frost remaining square cake with some of the red frosting.

5. Using wooden pick, draw area about 1 inch from top edge of round cake as shown. Frost area with red frosting.

6. Frost remaining round cake with white frosting and immediately decorate with gumballs.

7. Arrange pieces of black licorice around coin insertion area and place a foil-covered chocolate coin in center of area. Outline red cap with red licorice.
     Makes 16 to 20 servings

Color 1½ cups frosting red and ½ cup light gray; reserve 1½ cups white frosting.

Tip: For younger children, use marshmallows or soft candies for gumballs.

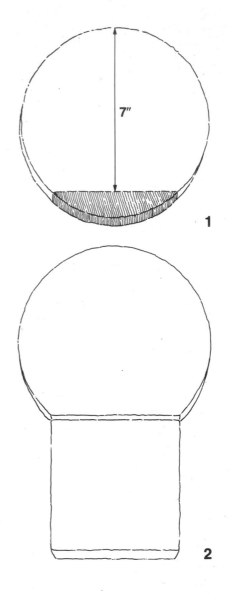

32

HAPPY FACE

CAKE & FROSTINGS

1 (9-inch) round cake
1 cup Base Frosting
(page 94), if desired
1¾ cups Buttercream Frosting
(page 95)*

EQUIPMENT

1 (10-inch) round cake
board, covered, or large
plate
Pastry bag and large
writing tip

1. Trim top of cake. Place on prepared cake board.

2. Frost entire cake with Base Frosting to seal in crumbs.

3. Frost again with yellow frosting.

4. Using writing tip and cocoa frosting, pipe eyes and mouth as shown in photo.

Makes 10 to 12 servings

Color 1½ cups frosting yellow. Mix ¼ cup frosting with 1 tablespoon unsweetened cocoa powder.

Variation: *Can also be made as a 2-layer cake. Use two 9-inch round cakes and 3½ cups frosting; decorate as above.*

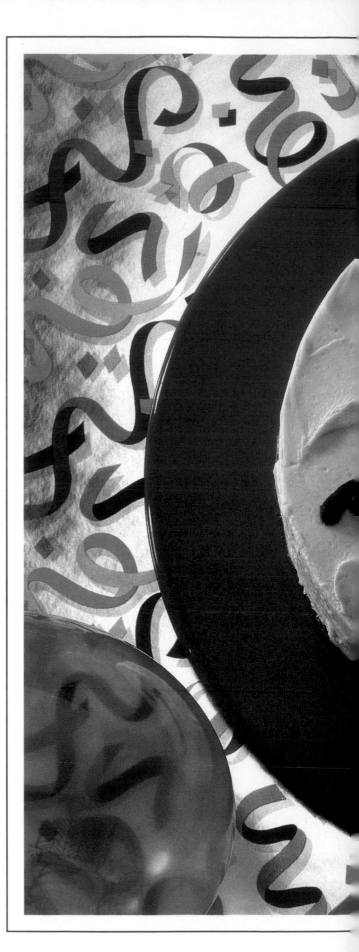

Hot Air Balloon

CAKES & FROSTINGS

2 (9-inch) round cakes
3 cups Buttercream Frosting
(page 95)*
1½ cups Base Frosting
(page 94), if desired

DECORATIONS & EQUIPMENT

Candy-coated chocolate
pieces
Chocolate sprinkles
2 black licorice twists
Small plastic animals, if
desired
1 (19×13-inch) cake board,
covered

1. Trim tops of cakes. Cut cakes
as shown in diagrams 1 and 2.

2. Position pieces on prepared
cake board as shown in diagram
3 and photo, connecting with
some of the yellow frosting.

3. Frost entire cake with Base
Frosting to seal in crumbs.

4. Frost balloon as shown in
photo. Decorate between colors
with chocolate pieces.

5. Frost basket with cocoa
frosting. Cover with chocolate
sprinkles.

6. Arrange licorice twists for
ropes.

7. Place plastic animals as
passengers, if desired.
Makes 14 to 16 servings

*Color 1¼ cups frosting yellow
and ½ cup blue; reserve ½ cup
white frosting. Mix remaining ¾
cup frosting with 1 tablespoon
unsweetened cocoa powder.*

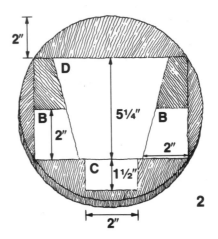

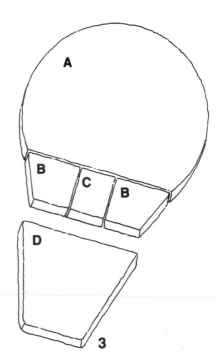

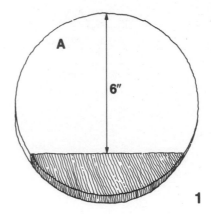

JACK-O-LANTERN

CAKES & FROSTINGS
   2 (10-inch) Bundt® cakes
5¼ cups Buttercream Frosting
      (page 95)*
   2 cups Base Frosting
      (page 94), if desired

DECORATIONS & EQUIPMENT
   Candy corn
   2 (10-inch) round cake
      boards, stacked and
      covered, or large plate
   1 (6-ounce) paper cup or ice
      cream wafer cone
   Pastry bag and medium
      writing tip

1. Trim flat sides of cakes. Place one cake on prepared cake board, flat-side up.

2. Frost top of cake with some of the orange frosting. Place second cake, flat-side down, over frosting.

3. Frost entire cake with Base Frosting to seal in crumbs.

4. Frost again with orange frosting.

5. Hold cup over fingers of one hand. Using other hand, frost cup with green frosting. Place upside-down in center of cake to form stem. Touch up frosting, if needed.

6. Using writing tip and brown frosting, pipe eyes and mouth. Arrange candy corn for teeth as shown in photo.

7. Before serving, remove stem. Slice and serve top cake first, then bottom.
   Makes 36 to 40 servings

Color 4½ cups frosting orange, ½ cup dark green and ¼ cup dark brown.

A fall birthday is the perfect opportunity for a party with a Halloween theme. Create scary decorations like spiderwebs and bats hanging from the ceiling and perhaps a coffin or graveyard scene. Turn down the lights and play a tape of scary sounds to add to the spooky atmosphere. Costumes are, of course, required but you may want to make masks as part of the party. Provide a plain mask for each child and supply plenty of paints, markers, construction paper, crepe paper, fabric, yarn and glitter. Stickers are also an easy way to decorate. Awards can be given for the scariest, prettiest or most creative—just be sure every child wins something.

JET PLANE

CAKE & FROSTINGS

- 1 (13×9-inch) cake
- 3½ cups Buttercream Frosting (page 95)*
- 1 cup Base Frosting (page 94), if desired

DECORATIONS & EQUIPMENT

- 4 pastel miniature marshmallows
- 1 small red gumdrop
- 1 (19×13-inch) cake board, cut to fit cake, if desired, and covered
- Pastry bag and medium writing tip

1. Trim top and edges of cake. Cut cake as shown in diagram 1.

2. Place piece A in center of prepared cake board. Frost top with some of the white frosting, then place piece B over frosting. Starting 3 inches from 1 side make an angled cut in piece B toward the front as shown in diagram 2.

3. Position remaining pieces on prepared cake board as shown in diagram 3, connecting with some of the white frosting. Trim sides to make nose about 1 inch wide. Trim top side edges of piece B to give a rounded appearance as shown in photo.

4. Frost entire cake with Base Frosting to seal in crumbs.

5. Using wooden pick, draw areas for windows as shown. Frost with light gray frosting.

6. Frost remaining cake with white frosting.

7. Using writing tip and blue frosting, pipe outlines for windows and design on wings as shown. Attach flattened marshmallows and gumdrop as shown.

Makes 14 to 16 servings

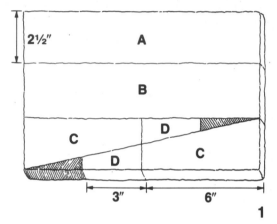

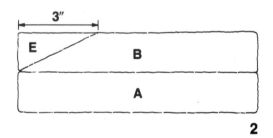

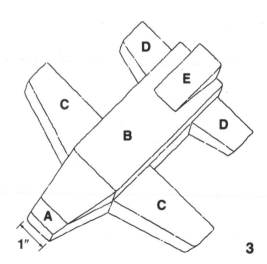

Color ½ cup frosting blue and ½ cup light gray; reserve 2½ cups white frosting.

40

LEGS THE CATERPILLAR

CAKES & FROSTING

6 medium (2¾-inch) cupcakes

1 jumbo (4-inch) cupcake

3½ cups Buttercream Frosting (page 95), colored yellow

DECORATIONS & EQUIPMENT

2 cups flaked coconut, tinted yellow to match frosting*

6 purple gumdrops

2 small purple candies or gumballs

2 small black licorice drops

1 black licorice whip
Red licorice whips

1 (19×13-inch) cake board, cut in half lengthwise and covered

1. Trim tops of cupcakes, if necessary. Frost sides and bottoms of medium cupcakes and roll in coconut, one at a time. Arrange, unfrosted-side down, in zigzag line on prepared cake board as shown in photo. Place gumdrops in center of each cupcake.

2. Frost side and bottom of jumbo cupcake. Roll in coconut, leaving one side plain for face. Place at front of cupcake line.

3. Arrange candies on large cupcake for face. Insert short pieces of the black licorice whip into centers of licorice drops for antennas; place as shown. Cut red licorice whips into small pieces and arrange as legs.

Makes 7 servings

To tint coconut, combine small amount of food coloring (paste or liquid) with 1 teaspoon water in large bowl. Add coconut and stir until evenly coated. Add more coloring, if needed.

Variation: More cupcakes can be added to serve more children. Add about ⅓ cup frosting and about ¼ cup flaked coconut for each additional cupcake.

A summer birthday is the perfect opportunity for an outdoor party. Have children dress for action and plan games that take advantage of the extra space outdoors. Team games like softball, soccer or volleyball are always fun. Or have the children compete in activities like running, jumping or throwing. Tug-of-war or a water balloon toss are classic outdoor games. Playing outside leads to hearty appetites so have substantial food prepared. Hot dogs and hamburgers with all the fixings are ideal along with generous servings of cake and ice cream.

LET'S PLAY BALL!

CAKES & FROSTINGS

- 1½ cups cake batter*
- 1 (9-inch) round cake*
- 1 recipe Jam Glaze (page 94), if desired
- 1½ cups Chocolate Buttercream Frosting (page 95)
- 2 cups Buttercream Frosting (page 95)**

DECORATIONS & EQUIPMENT

- 1 black licorice whip
- 1 (10-inch) round cake board, covered, or large plate
- Pastry bags, small and medium writing tips

1. Preheat oven to 350°F. Grease and flour 1-quart ovenproof bowl. Pour 1½ cups cake batter into prepared bowl. Bake 40 minutes or until wooden skewer inserted into center comes out clean. Let cool in bowl 10 minutes. Loosen edge; invert on wire rack and cool completely.

2. Trim top of round cake and flat side of bowl cake. Cut round cake as shown in diagram; place on prepared cake board.

3. Brush cake lightly with Jam Glaze. Let dry 1 hour.

4. Frost glove with chocolate frosting. Using medium writing tip and black frosting, pipe around edge of glove, forming fingers of glove as shown in photo.

5. Cut licorice whip into four 2-inch pieces. Crisscross across space between thumb and fingers of glove.

6. Place bowl cake on glove flat-side down. Frost with white frosting.

7. Using small writing tip and red frosting, pipe seams on baseball as shown.

Makes 16 to 18 servings

A 2-layer cake recipe or mix will yield enough batter for a 9-inch round cake and a bowl cake.

***Color ½ cup frosting black and ½ cup red; reserve 1 cup white frosting.*

Any die-hard sports fan would love a festive birthday party with a baseball theme. Be sure to include a complete ballpark menu with hot dogs and all the trimmings—popcorn, peanuts, cotton candy and ice-cold soda. Divide the guests into teams and play a game of baseball or test their knowledge of baseball trivia. Baseball cards or a baseball cap are fun favors.

LUCY THE LADYBUG

CAKE & FROSTINGS

4 cups cake batter*
1¾ cups Buttercream Frosting
(page 95)**

DECORATIONS & EQUIPMENT

Assorted candies
1 (10-inch) round cake
board, covered, or large
plate
Pastry bag and medium
writing tip

1. Preheat oven to 350°F. Grease and flour 2-quart ovenproof bowl. Pour 4 cups cake batter into prepared bowl. Bake 1 hour and 15 minutes or until wooden skewer inserted into center comes out clean. Cool 15 minutes in bowl. Loosen edge; invert on wire rack and cool completely.

2. Trim flat side of cake. Place on prepared cake board, flat-side down.

3. Using wooden pick, mark a semicircle about 3 inches from edge of cake for head as shown in photo.

4. Frost remainder of cake with red frosting. Frost head with cocoa frosting, reserving small portion for piping.

5. Using writing tip and reserved cocoa frosting, pipe line down center from head to other edge. Pipe line between the head and body.

6. Arrange assorted candies as shown.

Makes 14 to 18 servings

A 2-layer cake recipe or mix will yield about 4 cups cake batter.

****Color 1 cup frosting red. Mix ¾ cup frosting with 2 tablespoons unsweetened cocoa powder and 2 teaspoons milk.***

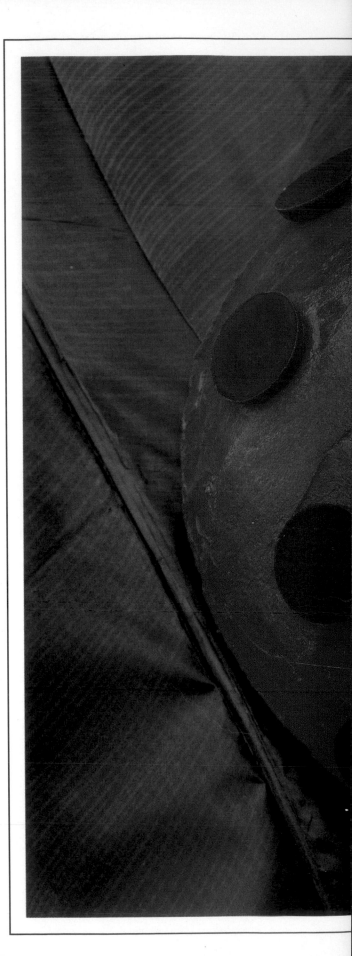

Ninja Turtle

CAKE & FROSTINGS

1 (9-inch) round cake
2¾ cups Buttercream Frosting (page 95)*
1 cup Base Frosting (page 94), if desired

DECORATIONS & EQUIPMENT

2 black jelly beans
Blue ribbon
1 (10-inch) round cake board, covered, or large plate
Pastry bags and medium writing tip

1. Place knife on cake edge, ¾ inch down. Make wedge cut (piece A) by moving the knife up and toward the center as shown in diagram 1. Attach piece A to uncut side with some of the green frosting, placing thin edge near the center as shown in diagram 2.

2. Place cake on prepared cake board. Frost entire cake with Base Frosting to seal in crumbs.

3. Using wooden pick, draw mask as shown in photo, continuing down sides of cake. Frost with blue frosting. Frost remainder of cake with green frosting, mounding nose area.

4. Using writing tip and dark gray frosting, pipe mouth. Use spoon to add red frosting as shown.

5. Pipe light gray frosting into ovals for eyes. Add jelly beans.

6. Attach small pieces of blue ribbon to side of cake for ends of mask.

Makes 10 to 12 servings

Color 1½ cups frosting green, ½ cup blue, ¼ cup dark gray, ¼ cup light gray and 1 tablespoon red.

Variation: Can be made as a 2-layer cake. Use 2 (9-inch) round cakes and increase green frosting to 2½ cups; decorate as above.

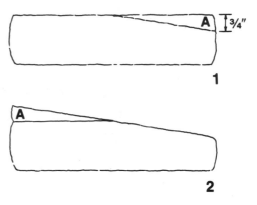

P.C. THE COMPUTER

CAKES & FROSTINGS

   1 (9-inch) square cake
   1 (13×9-inch) cake
   3 cups Buttercream Frosting
     (page 95)*
1½ cups Base Frosting
     (page 94), if desired

DECORATIONS & EQUIPMENT

  Pastel candy-coated
    chocolate pieces
1 white sugar wafer cookie
1 (19×13-inch) cake board,
    cut in half crosswise
    and covered
  Pastry bag and medium
    writing tip

1. Trim tops and edges of cakes. Cut 2 inches from one side of square cake. Place on prepared cake board.

2. Cut 13×9-inch cake in half crosswise. Frost top of 1 half with some of the light green frosting. Place remaining half on frosting. Position upright against square cake as shown in diagram, connecting with some of the light green frosting. Insert wooden picks or small wooden skewers for additional support, if needed.

3. Frost entire cake with Base Frosting to seal in crumbs.

4. Using wooden pick, draw area for screen, about 1½ inches from edges, as shown in photo. Frost screen with white frosting.

5. Frost remaining cake with light green frosting. Arrange rows of chocolate pieces and wafer cookie for keyboard.

6. Using writing tip and dark green frosting, pipe an outline around white area and "Happy Birthday" on screen.

7. To serve, remove wooden picks. Lay upright part of cake flat before cutting.
Makes 28 to 32 servings

*Color 2 cups frosting light green and ½ cup dark green; reserve ½ cup white frosting.

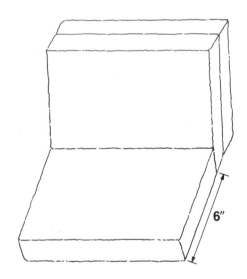

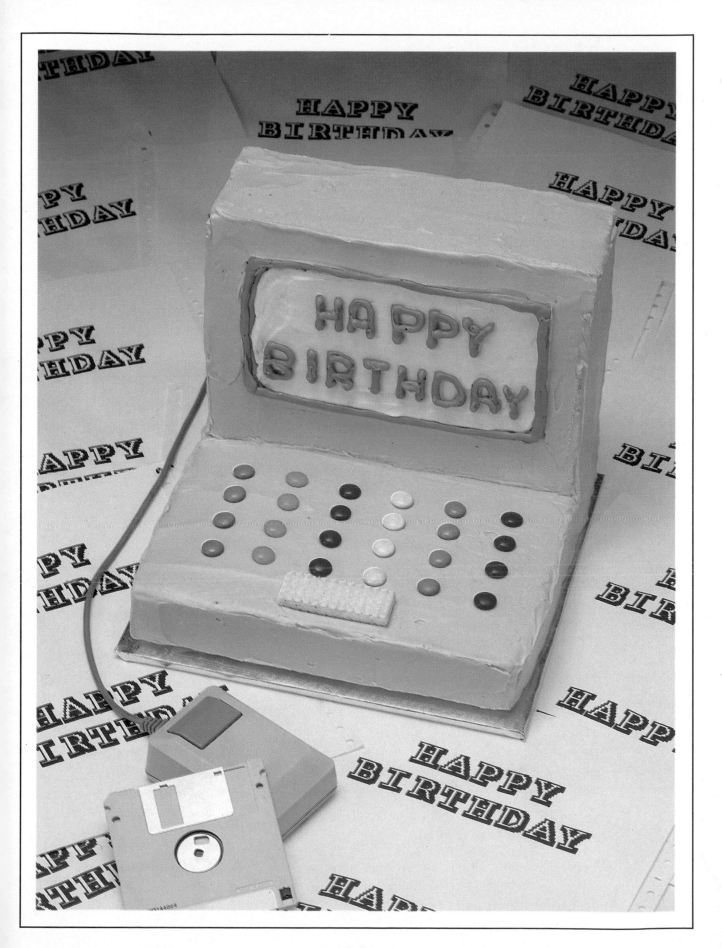

PICK-UP TRUCK

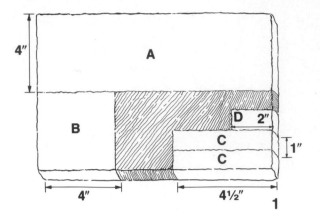

CAKE & FROSTINGS

1 (13×9-inch) cake
2½ cups Buttercream Frosting
(page 95)*
1 cup Base Frosting
(page 94), if desired

DECORATIONS & EQUIPMENT

1 black licorice whip
4 chocolate sandwich
cookies
4 large nonpareils
Jelly beans
1 (19×13-inch) cake board,
cut in half lengthwise or
to fit cake, if desired,
and covered
**Pastry bag and medium
writing tip**

1. Trim top and edges of cake. Cut as shown in diagram 1. Place piece A on prepared cake board. Frost top of piece A with some of the yellow frosting.

2. Place piece B on piece A about 3½ inches in from short end as shown in diagram 2. Position remaining pieces on piece A as shown in diagram 2, connecting with some of the yellow frosting.

3. Frost entire cake with Base Frosting to seal in crumbs.

4. Frost 3 sides of piece B with white frosting for windows.

5. Frost remainder of cake with yellow frosting, reserving small portion for piping.

6. Using writing tip and reserved yellow frosting, pipe border around windows as shown in photo. Cut licorice whip into pieces and place on windshield for wipers. Position cookies for wheels. Attach nonpareils for lights and place jelly beans in bed of truck.

Makes 10 to 14 servings

***Color 2 cups frosting yellow;
reserve ½ cup white frosting.***

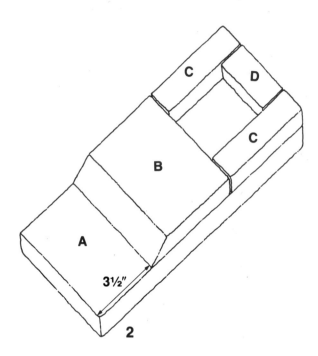

PRACTICALLY PIZZA

CAKE & FROSTINGS

1 (9-inch) round cake
1 cup Base Frosting
    (page 94), if desired
1¾ cups Buttercream Frosting
    (page 95)*
1¼ cups Uncooked Fondant
    (page 94)**

EQUIPMENT

1 (10-inch) round cake
    board, covered, or small
    pizza pan or wooden
    board
Pastry bag and extra large
    writing tip

1. Trim top of cake. Place cake on prepared cake board.

2. Frost entire cake with Base Frosting to seal in crumbs.

3. Frost side of cake and 1-inch rim with some of the cocoa frosting.

4. Frost remainder of cake with red frosting.

5. Using writing tip and remaining cocoa frosting, pipe around rim for raised crust. Flatten slightly with back of spoon.

6. For olives, roll green fondant to rectangle about ¾ inch wide and ¼ inch thick. Form red fondant into log about ¼ inch in diameter. Place red fondant on one long edge of green fondant; roll up jelly-roll style. Seal edges. Refrigerate until firm. Cut crosswise into thin slices and flatten slightly.

7. For pepperoni, knead reddish-brown fondant and 1 tablespoon white fondant together lightly (some white should still be visible). Form into roll about 1 inch in diameter. Refrigerate until firm. Cut crosswise into thin slices.

8. For cheese, shape remaining white fondant into log, about 1½ inches in diameter. Refrigerate until very firm. Using cheese shredder, shred fondant over pizza.

9. Arrange olives and pepperoni on pizza.

Makes 10 to 12 servings

Tip: Use rolled green and white gumdrops (see page 28) cut into small pieces for chopped bell pepper and onion.

***Color 1 cup frosting red. Mix ¾ cup frosting with 2 teaspoons unsweetened cocoa powder.**

****Color 3 tablespoons fondant olive green, ¼ cup reddish-brown and 1 tablespoon red; reserve ¾ cup white fondant.**

PRINCESS DOLL

CAKES & FROSTINGS

4 cups cake batter*
1 (8-inch) round cake
3 cups Buttercream Frosting (page 95), colored peach
1 cup Base Frosting (page 94), if desired

DECORATIONS & EQUIPMENT

Pastel miniature marshmallows
Small chocolate nonpareils
1 (10-inch) round cake board, covered, or large plate
1 doll body and head**

1. Preheat oven to 350°F. Grease and flour 2-quart ovenproof bowl. Pour 4 cups cake batter into prepared bowl. Bake 1 hour and 15 minutes or until wooden skewer inserted into center comes out clean. Cool 15 minutes in bowl. Loosen edge; invert on wire rack and cool completely.

2. Trim flat side of bowl cake and top of round cake. Trim round cake even with bowl cake. Place round cake on prepared cake board. Frost top with some of the peach frosting. Place bowl cake, flat-side down, on frosting.

3. Frost entire cake with Base Frosting to seal in crumbs.

A 2-layer cake recipe or mix will yield about 4 cups cake batter.

**Doll body and head can be purchased from stores carrying cake decorating supplies or use doll with legs removed or covered in plastic wrap.*

4. Make small V-shaped hole in center of cake; insert doll in hole. (To keep doll's clothing clean, wrap bottom of doll in plastic wrap.)

5. Frost cake with peach frosting. Decorate skirt with flattened marshmallows as shown in photo. Decorate bottom of skirt with chocolate nonpareils.

6. To serve, remove doll and slice cake into small wedges.
Makes 14 to 18 servings

Use the Princess Doll cake as a charming centerpiece for an elegant birthday tea party. Have all the guests bring along their favorite doll (you may even want to include a separate miniature invitation for the doll). Ask everyone to dress up for the occasion. Set the table with china and linens. Serve milk or juice from a teapot along with fancy finger sandwiches or cookies. You can act as the maid or butler by taking coats, announcing the guests (and accompanying dolls) as they arrive, and serving the meal. Party favors may include fancy hair ribbons (for guests and dolls) or doll clothes and accessories.

RADIO FUN

CAKE & FROSTINGS

- 1 (9-inch) square cake
- 1 cup Base Frosting (page 94), if desired
- 3 cups Buttercream Frosting (page 95)*

DECORATIONS & EQUIPMENT

- Pink and black licorice pieces
- 2 yellow candy discs
- 1 orange flat gumdrop
- 1 (19×13-inch) cake board, cut into 10×10-inch square and covered
- Icing comb
- Pastry bags, small writing tip and basketweave tip

1. Trim top and edges of cake. Cut as shown in diagram.

2. Place cake on prepared cake board.

3. Frost entire cake with Base Frosting to seal in crumbs.

4. Frost as shown in photo, reserving small portion of each color for piping. While frosting is soft, use icing comb as shown in photo below to make design for speaker.**

5. Using flat side of basketweave tip and reserved yellow frosting, pipe two vertical lines, one at end of speaker section and another 2 inches from the first line.

6. Using writing tip and reserved green frosting, pipe accents on handle as shown.

7. Position candies as shown.
Makes 10 to 14 servings

Color 2 cups frosting green and 1 cup yellow.

Design on speaker can also be made with fork.

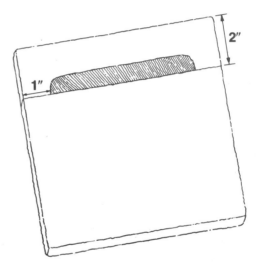

58

REX THE DINOSAUR

CAKE & FROSTINGS

1 (13×9-inch) cake
2 cups Buttercream Frosting
  (page 95), colored green
1 recipe Jam Glaze (page 94)

DECORATIONS & EQUIPMENT

Assorted candies
1 (19×13-inch) cake board,
  cut to fit cake, if desired,
  and covered

1. Trim top and edges of cake. Using diagram 1 as guide, draw pattern pieces on 13×9-inch piece of waxed paper. Cut pattern out and place on cake. Cut out dinosaur pieces.

2. Position pieces on prepared cake board as shown in diagram 2, connecting with some of the green frosting.

3. Brush cake lightly with Jam Glaze. Let dry about 1 hour.

4. Frost cake with green frosting.

5. Decorate with assorted candies as shown in photo.

Makes 8 to 10 servings

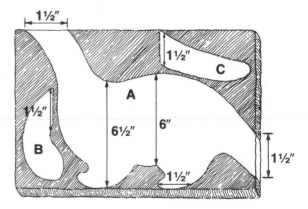

1

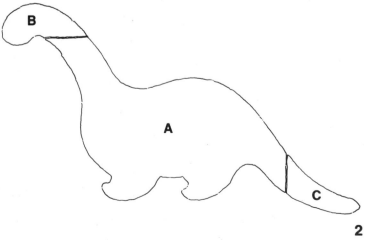

ROBBIE THE ROBOT

CAKES & FROSTINGS

1 (9-inch) round cake
1 (8-inch) square cake
3½ cups Buttercream Frosting (page 95)*
1 cup Base Frosting (page 94), if desired

DECORATIONS & EQUIPMENT

Assorted candies or gumballs
Pink and white sugar wafer cookies
1 (19×13-inch) cake board, cut in half crosswise and covered
Pastry bags and basketweave tip

1. Trim tops and edges of cakes. Cut round cake as shown in diagram 1.

2. Position pieces on prepared cake board as shown in diagram 2, connecting with some of the blue frosting. Trim sides of round cake to match sides of square cake, if necessary.

3. Frost entire cake with Base Frosting to seal in crumbs.

4. Using wooden pick, draw line across cake 1 inch up from bottom. Frost area with some of the white frosting as shown in photo. Frost remaining square cake with some of the blue frosting.

5. Draw line 4 inches above frosted blue area. Frost area with gray frosting.

6. Divide remaining area in half vertically; frost areas with blue and white frosting as shown, reserving small portion of each color for piping.

7. Using flat side of basketweave tip and reserved white frosting, pipe vertical line dividing white and blue frosting.

8. Using flat side of basketweave tip and reserved blue frosting, pipe border between blue and gray frosting as shown.

9. Decorate with assorted candies and wafer cookies as shown.

Makes 16 to 20 servings

Color 1½ cups frosting blue and 1 cup gray; reserve 1 cup white frosting.

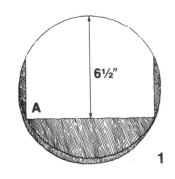

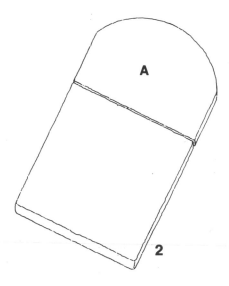

62

SAILBOAT

CAKE & FROSTINGS

   1 (13×9-inch) cake
3½ cups Buttercream Frosting
     (page 95)*
   1 cup Base Frosting
     (page 94), if desired

DECORATIONS & EQUIPMENT

   5 white licorice drops or
     gumballs
   1 black licorice twist
   1 black licorice whip
     Small flag, if desired
   1 (19×13-inch) cake board,
     cut to fit cake, if desired,
     and covered

1. Trim top and edges of cake.
Cut as shown in diagram 1.

2. Position pieces on prepared
cake board as shown in diagram
2, connecting with some of the
green frosting.

3. Frost entire cake with Base
Frosting to seal in crumbs.

4. Frost again as shown in photo.

5. Arrange candies as shown.
Place flag on top.
    Makes 12 to 14 servings

***Color 1½ cups frosting green
and 1¼ cups peach; reserve
¾ cup white frosting.***

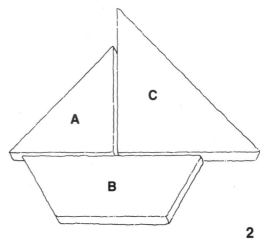

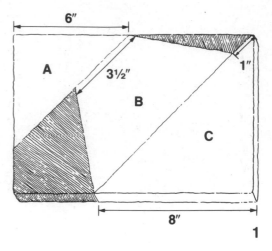

SKATEBOARD

CAKES & FROSTINGS

    1 (9-inch) round cake
    1 (13×9-inch) cake
3½ cups Buttercream Frosting
      (page 95)*
1½ cups Base Frosting
      (page 94), if desired

DECORATIONS & EQUIPMENT

    5 green jelly beans
    5 purple jelly beans
    8 chocolate sandwich
      cookies
    1 (19×13-inch) cake board
      Foot-shaped cookie cutter
      Pastry bags, medium
        writing tip and
        basketweave tip

1. Trim tops and edges of cakes. Cut round cake in half crosswise. Frost top of one half with some of the orange frosting. Place remaining half on frosting. Starting from round side, near top of cake, make an angled cut almost to bottom layer to form wedge as shown in diagram 1.

2. Cut cakes as shown in diagram 2.

3. Using diagram 2 as a guide, draw shape of cake on cake board. Cut cake board slightly smaller and cover.

4. Place cakes on prepared cake board as shown in diagram 3, connecting with some of the orange frosting.

5. Frost entire cake with Base Frosting to seal in crumbs.

6. Frost again with orange frosting. Using cookie cutter or wooden pick, draw outlines of feet as shown in photo. Using writing tip and green and purple frostings, pipe around outlines of feet. Place jelly beans on feet for toes.

7. Using plain side of basketweave tip, pipe white frosting as shown.

8. Connect cookies in pairs with white frosting to make 4 sets of wheels. Lay each pair flat on cutting board and cut small amount off tops and bottoms of cookies to form flat edges.

9. Use frosting to attach wheels to underside of cake board.
Makes 20 to 24 servings

Tip: Set skateboard on tray when moving. For easier serving, remove wheels before cutting.

*Color 2½ cups frosting orange, ¼ cup green and ¼ cup purple; reserve ½ cup white frosting.

1

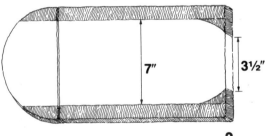

7"

3½"

2

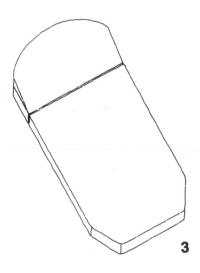

3

SNOWY THE SNOWMAN

CAKES & FROSTINGS

- 2 (9-inch) round cakes*
- 1 medium cupcake
- 3½ cups Buttercream Frosting (page 95)**
- 1½ cups Base Frosting (page 94), if desired

DECORATIONS & EQUIPMENT

- 3 cups flaked coconut
- 2 large black gumdrops Assorted candies
- 2 (10-inch) round cake boards, taped together and covered, or large tray

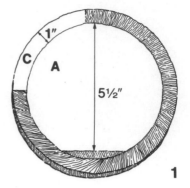

1. Trim tops of cakes. Cut as shown in diagrams 1 and 2.

2. Position pieces on prepared cake board as shown in diagram 3, connecting with some of the white frosting.

3. Frost entire cake with Base Frosting to seal in crumbs.

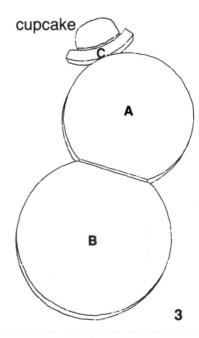

4. Frost again with white frosting. Cover with coconut. Frost hat with gray frosting.

5. Cut a thin slice off each black gumdrop; use for eyes. Arrange assorted candies as shown in photo.

Makes 14 to 16 servings

Before baking round cakes, reserve enough batter for 1 cupcake.

**Color ½ cup frosting dark gray or black; reserve 3 cups white frosting.*

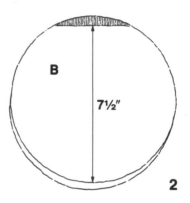

SOCCER BALL

CAKE & FROSTINGS
4 cups cake batter*
1 cup Base Frosting
   (page 94), if desired
2½ cups Buttercream Frosting
   (page 95)

DECORATIONS & EQUIPMENT
Red licorice whips
Red colored sugar
1 (10-inch) round cake
   board, covered, or large
   plate

1. Preheat oven to 350°F. Grease and flour 2½- to 3-quart ovenproof bowl. Pour cake batter into prepared bowl. Bake 1 hour and 15 minutes or until wooden skewer inserted into center comes out clean. Cool 15 minutes in bowl. Loosen edge; invert on wire rack and cool completely.

2. Trim flat side of cake. Place on prepared cake board. Trim edges into ball shape.

3. Frost entire cake with Base Frosting to seal in crumbs. Frost again with white frosting.

4. Using wooden pick, draw a pentagon (with five 1½-inch sides) in center of top of cake. Surround pentagon with five hexagons (each with six 1½-inch sides). Repeat pattern alternating pentagons and hexagons to cover entire ball as shown in photo.

5. Cut licorice whips into 1½-inch pieces. Outline shapes with licorice. Fill pentagon shapes with colored sugar.
   Makes 14 to 16 servings

A 2-layer cake recipe or mix will yield about 4 cups cake batter.

Variation: Color additional 1 cup of frosting bright blue. Using extra large writing tip and blue frosting, pipe frosting inside pentagon shapes, then smooth with small spatula.

SPACE SHUTTLE 🕯🕯🕯

CAKES & FROSTINGS

- 1 (13×9-inch) cake
- 1 (9-inch) square cake
- 3 cups Buttercream Frosting (page 95)*
- 1½ cups Base Frosting (page 94), if desired

EQUIPMENT

- 1 (19×13-inch) cake board, cut to fit cake, if desired, and covered
- Pastry bag and medium writing tip

1. Trim tops and edges of cakes. Cut 13×9-inch cake as shown in diagram 1. Cut square cake as shown in diagram 2.

2. Place piece A in center of prepared cake board. Frost top with some of the white frosting. Place piece B over frosting as shown in diagram 3.

3. Starting 3½ inches from 1 side make an angled cut toward front to form nose, cutting through top and some of bottom layer as shown in diagram 3.

4. Position remaining pieces on prepared cake board as shown in diagram 4, connecting with some of the white frosting. Trim sides to make nose about 1 inch wide.

5. Frost entire cake with Base Frosting to seal in crumbs.

6. Using wooden pick, draw areas for window and nose as shown in photo. Frost window with light gray frosting. Frost nose with dark gray frosting, reserving small portion for piping. Frost remaining areas with white frosting.

7. Using writing tip and reserved dark gray frosting, pipe stripes on wings and tail and outline window as shown. Pipe "USA" on wings.

Makes 14 to 16 servings

*Color ¼ cup frosting light gray and ¼ cup dark gray or black; reserve 2½ cups white frosting.

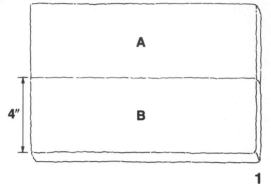

1

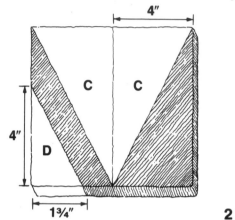

2

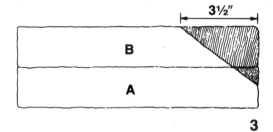

3

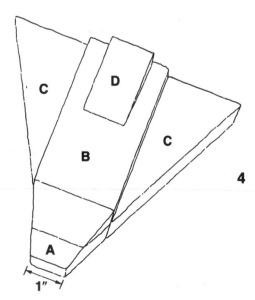

4

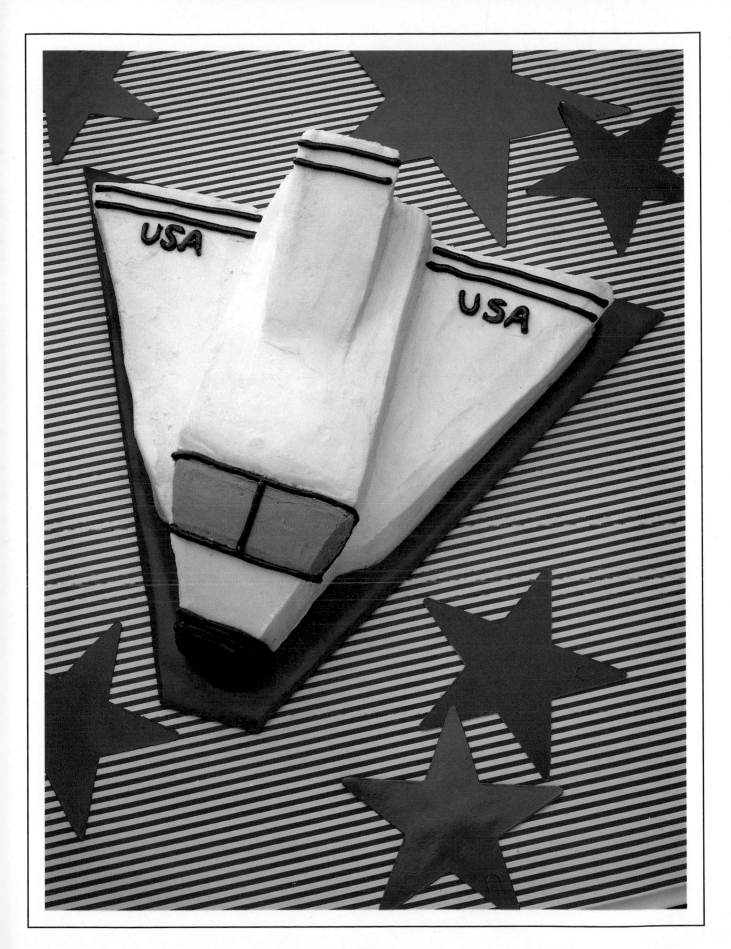

SPEEDY RACETRACK

CAKES & FROSTINGS

- 1 (9-inch) round cake
- 1 (13×9-inch) cake
- 3½ cups Buttercream Frosting (page 95)*
- 1½ cups Base Frosting (page 94), if desired

DECORATIONS & EQUIPMENT

- Green colored sugar
- 2 to 3 rolls white donut-shaped hard candies, cut in half
- ½ (16-ounce) box cinnamon graham crackers
- 2- to 3-inch race cars
- Flags, if desired
- 1 (19×13-inch) cake board, cut to fit cake, if desired, and covered

1. Trim tops and edges of cakes. Cut round cake in half crosswise. Cut 13×9-inch cake as shown in diagram 1.

2. Position pieces on prepared cake board as shown in diagram 2, connecting with some of the green frosting.

3. Frost entire cake with Base Frosting to seal in crumbs.

4. Using wooden pick, draw area for track, about 2 inches wide, as shown in photo. Frost center of cake with green frosting. Sprinkle with colored sugar. Frost track and sides of cake with cocoa frosting.

5. Arrange hard candies, cut-side down, around inside of track. Cut graham crackers about ¼ inch higher than cake. Arrange around edge of cake, attaching with more cocoa frosting, if needed.

6. Let frosting harden before placing cars and flags on track.
Makes 20 to 24 servings

Mix 2 cups frosting with 2 tablespoons unsweetened cocoa powder. Color 1½ cups green.

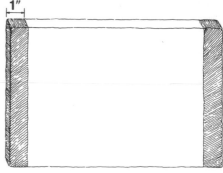

1″

1

2

STRAWBERRY ICE CREAM CONE

CAKES & FROSTINGS

 1 (9-inch) round cake
 1 (13×9-inch) cake
3½ cups Buttercream Frosting
     (page 95)*
 2 cups Base Frosting
     (page 94), if desired

DECORATIONS & EQUIPMENT

  Red gumdrops, cut in
     small pieces
 1 (19×13-inch) cake board,
     cut to fit cake, if
     desired, and covered
  Pastry bag and
     basketweave tip

1. Trim tops and edges of cakes. Cut cakes as shown in diagram 1.

2. Position pieces on prepared cake board as shown in diagram 2, connecting with some of the pink frosting.

3. Frost entire cake with Base Frosting to seal in crumbs.

4. Frost round cake with pink frosting. Arrange small pieces of gumdrops in frosting.

5. Frost cone with cocoa frosting, reserving ½ cup. Using basketweave tip and reserved frosting, pipe as shown in photo.
Makes 18 to 22 servings

Mix 2 cups frosting with ¼ cup unsweetened cocoa powder; color 1½ cups frosting pink.

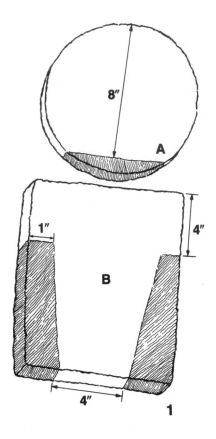

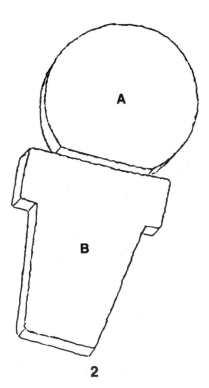

TEDDY BEAR TRAIN

CAKE & FROSTINGS

1 (13×9-inch) cake
6 cups Buttercream Frosting
   (page 95)*
3 cups Base Frosting
   (page 94), if desired

DECORATIONS & EQUIPMENT

1 large marshmallow
1 round chocolate candy
   Teddy bear cookies or
      animal crackers
   Assorted candies and
      cookies
32 chocolate discs
   Flat wooden craft sticks
1 (19×13-inch) cake board,
   cut in half lengthwise,
   short ends taped
   together, and covered
   Non-toxic glue

1. Arrange wooden sticks equal distance apart on covered cake board. Glue in place.

2. Trim top and edges of cake.

3. Cut cake as shown in diagram 1.

4. Place piece A on top of 1 of the other pieces, connecting with some of the red frosting as shown in diagram 2.

5. Frost sides and tops of pieces with Base Frosting to seal in crumbs.

6. Frost engine with red frosting. Place large marshmallow on engine and top with chocolate candy as shown in photo.

7. Frost remaining pieces with each of the different colors. Press cookies onto sides.

8. Using spatula, carefully place cars on track, starting with the engine and spacing evenly apart. Arrange assorted candies and cookies on top of each car. Arrange 4 chocolate discs, 2 per side, on each car for wheels as shown.

Makes 14 to 16 servings

*Color ¾ cup frosting _each_ red, medium blue, yellow, orange, green, pink, purple and dark blue.

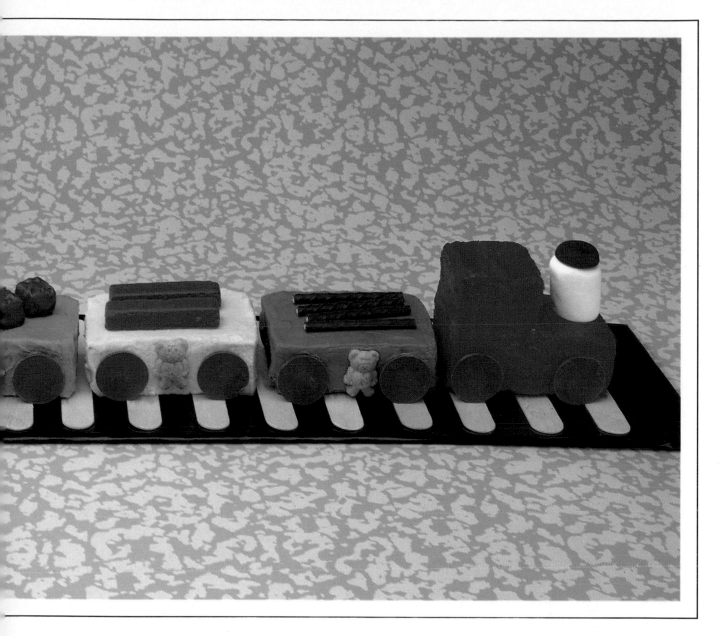

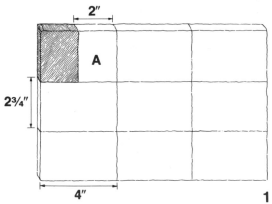

2″

A

2¾″

4″

1

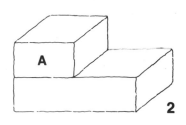

A

2

TELLY PHONE

CAKE & FROSTINGS

- 1 (13×9-inch) cake
- 1 cup Base Frosting (page 94), if desired
- 2 cups Buttercream Frosting (page 95)*

DECORATIONS & EQUIPMENT

- Pink colored sugar
- Assorted candies
- 1 (19×13-inch) cake board, cut in half crosswise and covered
- Pastry bag and small writing tip

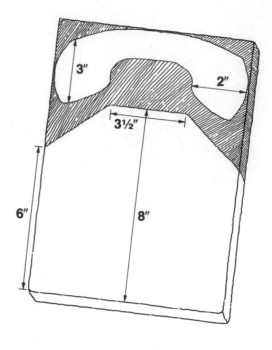

1. Trim top and edges of cake. Cut as shown in diagram.

2. Position pieces on prepared cake board as shown in photo.

3. Frost entire cake with Base Frosting to seal in crumbs.

4. Using wooden pick, draw 5-inch circle for dial area as shown in photo. Frost area with white frosting, reserving small portion for piping.

5. Frost remaining cake with purple frosting; sprinkle with colored sugar.

6. Using writing tip and reserved frosting, pipe line around dial as shown.

7. Decorate cake with assorted candies as shown.

Makes 10 to 14 servings

*Color 1½ cups frosting purple; reserve ½ cup white frosting.

For lots of silly fun try the telephone game. Here's how it's played: Everybody sits in a circle. One person starts a secret message (you may want to supply the messages) and whispers it to the person on his or her right. That person must pass the message on to the next person and so on around the circle. No repeating the message. Do your best to hear it on the first try. The last person in the circle must say the message they heard out loud—it is often quite different from the original.

TIC-TAC-TOE

CAKE & FROSTINGS

1 (8-inch) square cake
1 cup Base Frosting
   (page 94), if desired
1½ cups Buttercream Frosting
   (page 95)

DECORATIONS & EQUIPMENT

4 black licorice twists
3 large red gumdrops
24 small red candies
1 (19×13-inch) cake board,
   cut in half crosswise
   and covered, or large
   plate

1. Trim top and edges of cake. Place on prepared cake board.

2. Frost entire cake with Base Frosting to seal in crumbs.

3. Frost again with buttercream frosting.

4. Using wooden pick, mark cake into thirds, both horizontally and vertically. Arrange 2 licorice twists over horizontal lines; cut and place remaining licorice twists as shown in photo.

5. Decorate with gumdrops and candies as shown.

Makes 9 to 12 servings

TOUCHDOWN FOOTBALL

CAKE & FROSTINGS

1 (13×9-inch) cake
3½ cups Chocolate
    Buttercream Frosting
    (page 95)
1 recipe Jam Glaze
    (page 94), if desired

DECORATIONS & EQUIPMENT

Black licorice whips
Red candy-coated
    chocolate pieces
Purchased "Happy
    Birthday" decoration
1 (10-inch) round cake
    board, cut to fit cake, if
    desired, and covered, or
    large plate

1. Trim top and edges of cake.
Cut cake in half crosswise. Frost
top of one half with some of the
chocolate frosting. Place
remaining half on frosting.

2. Cut football shape as shown in
diagram. Brush cake lightly with
Jam Glaze. Let dry 1 hour.

3. Frost with chocolate frosting,
mounding frosting slightly on top.

4. Decorate as shown in photo,
using licorice for laces.

Makes 10 to 14 servings

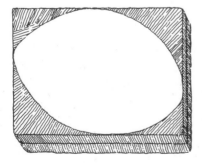

T-RIFFIC BIRTHDAY T-SHIRT

CAKE & FROSTINGS

1 (13×9-inch) cake
3½ cups Buttercream Frosting (page 95)*
1 cup Base Frosting (page 94), if desired

DECORATIONS & EQUIPMENT

Assorted candies and sprinkles
1 (19×13-inch) cake board, cut into 14×13-inch rectangle, if desired, and covered
Heart-shaped cookie cutter
Pastry bag and medium writing tip

1. Trim top and edges of cake. Cut as shown in diagram 1.

2. Position pieces on prepared cake board as shown in diagram 2, connecting with some of the yellow frosting.

3. Frost entire cake with Base Frosting to seal in crumbs.

4. Frost again with yellow frosting. Decorate neck with assorted candies.

5. Using cookie cutter, make outline on T-shirt; fill with sprinkles. Using wooden pick, write "Happy Birthday" as shown in photo.

6. Using writing tip and red frosting, pipe outline of heart and letters.

Makes 14 to 16 servings

Color 3 cups frosting yellow and ½ cup red.

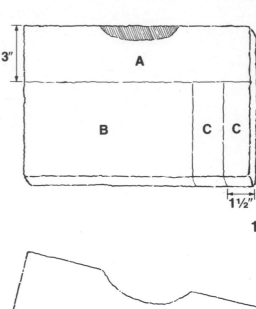

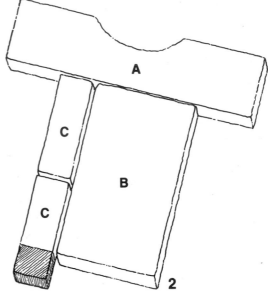

86

WEBSTER'S WEB

CAKE & FROSTINGS

- 1 (9-inch) round cake
- 1 cup Base Frosting (page 94), if desired
- 2 cups Buttercream Frosting (page 95)*

DECORATIONS & EQUIPMENT

- 2 black licorice candies or jelly beans
- 1 black licorice whip
- 1 (10-inch) round cake board, covered, or large plate
    Pastry bag and medium writing tip

1. Trim top of cake. Place on prepared cake board.

2. Frost entire cake with Base Frosting to seal in crumbs.

3. Frost again with blue frosting.

4. Using writing tip and white frosting, pipe 4 concentric circles, about 1 inch apart, and a dot in the center of the cake. Using spatula or tip of knife, draw through circles at regular intervals as shown in photo below, *alternating direction each time.*

5. Place candies for spider's body and head on cake. Cut 8 licorice whip pieces; curve and arrange for legs.

Makes 10 to 12 servings

*Color 1½ cups frosting blue; reserve ½ cup white frosting.

Variation: Can also be made as a 2-layer cake. Use two 9-inch round cakes and increase blue frosting to 2½ cups; decorate as above.

Play a game of spiderwebs with the children at this party. You'll need a ball of colored yarn for each child at the party. (It is easier to play if there is a different color for each child.) Before the party begins, tie a prize to the end of each ball of yarn and hide the prize. Then unwind the balls of yarn all around a room—around the furniture, under tables, behind the sofa—creating a spiderweb of colored yarn. When the party starts, pass out the loose ends of yarn to the children. Have them wind the yarn back up into a ball, following it all around the room until they find the prize.

WUZZY THE BEAR

CAKES & FROSTINGS

2 (9-inch) round cakes
2¼ cups Chocolate
    Buttercream Frosting
    (page 95)
1 recipe Jam Glaze
    (page 94), if desired
1¼ cups Buttercream Frosting
    (page 95)*

DECORATIONS & EQUIPMENT

Chocolate sprinkles
Assorted candies
2 large yellow gumdrops
1 large red gumdrop
1 (19×13-inch) cake board,
    cut into 13×13-inch
    square and covered

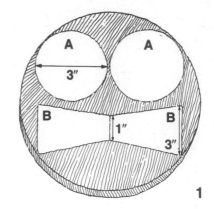

1. Trim tops of cakes; place one cake on prepared cake board. Cut remaining cake as shown in diagram 1.

2. Position pieces on prepared cake board as shown in diagram 2, connecting with some of the chocolate frosting.

3. Brush cake lightly with Jam Glaze. Let dry 1 hour.

4. Using wooden pick, draw 4-inch circle for face as shown in photo. Frost bear, except for face and bow tie, with chocolate frosting; sprinkle with chocolate sprinkles.

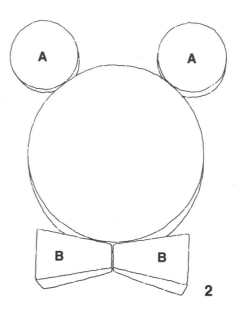

5. Frost face with white frosting. Frost the bow tie with blue frosting and decorate with assorted candies as shown.

6. Roll out gumdrops for eyes and tongue.**

7. Decorate face as shown, using frosting to attach eyes, nose and tongue, if needed.

     Makes 12 to 16 servings

*Color ¾ cup frosting blue; reserve ½ cup white frosting.

**See tip on rolling gumdrops, page 28.

BASIC CAKES & FROSTINGS

Use the following baking times when preparing any of the cakes in this chapter:

- 1 (13×9-inch) cake: 35 to 40 minutes
- 1 (10-inch) Bundt® cake: 45 to 55 minutes
- 2 (9-inch) cakes: 35 to 40 minutes
- 2 (8-inch) squares: 30 to 35 minutes
- 3 (8-inch) rounds: 20 to 25 minutes
- 8 large (4-inch) cupcakes: 35 to 40 minutes
- 24 medium (2¾-inch) cupcakes: 20 to 25 minutes

WHITE CAKE

2¼ cups all-purpose flour
1 tablespoon baking powder
½ teaspoon salt
1⅔ cups sugar
½ cup butter or margarine, softened
1 cup milk
2 teaspoons vanilla
3 egg whites

Preheat oven to 350°F. Grease and flour cake pan(s) or grease and line with waxed paper. Sift flour, baking powder and salt together in large bowl. Stir in sugar. Add butter, milk and vanilla; beat with electric mixer at low speed 30 seconds. Beat at medium speed 2 minutes. Add egg whites; beat 2 minutes. Pour into prepared cake pan(s) and bake as directed above, until wooden pick inserted into center comes out clean. Cool in pan 10 minutes. Loosen cake edge from pan, invert on a rack, remove waxed paper and cool completely.

YELLOW BUTTER CAKE

2 cups all-purpose flour
4 teaspoons baking powder
½ teaspoon salt
1½ cups sugar
½ cup butter or margarine, softened
1 cup milk
1 teaspoon vanilla
3 eggs

Preheat oven to 350°F. Grease and flour cake pan(s) or grease and line with waxed paper. Sift flour, baking powder and salt together in large bowl. Stir in sugar. Add butter, milk and vanilla and beat with electric mixer at low speed 30 seconds. Beat at medium speed 2 minutes. Add eggs; beat 2 minutes. Pour into prepared cake pan(s) and bake as directed on page 92, until wooden pick inserted into center comes out clean. Cool in pan 10 minutes. Loosen cake edge from pan, invert on a rack, remove waxed paper and cool completely.

CHOCOLATE CAKE

2 cups all-purpose flour
⅔ cup unsweetened cocoa powder
1¾ teaspoons baking soda
½ teaspoon baking powder
½ teaspoon salt
1¾ cups sugar
⅔ cup shortening
1 cup cold water
2 teaspoons vanilla
3 eggs

Preheat oven to 350°F. Grease and flour cake pan(s) or grease and line with waxed paper. Sift flour, cocoa, baking soda, baking powder, and salt together in large bowl. Stir in sugar. Add shortening. Gradually beat in water at low speed with electric mixer until combined. Stir in vanilla. Beat at high speed 2 minutes. Add eggs; beat 2 minutes. Pour into prepared cake pan(s) and bake as directed on page 92, until wooden pick inserted into center comes out clean. Cool in pan 10 minutes. Loosen cake edge from pan, invert on a rack, remove waxed paper and cool completely.

To save time, bake cakes ahead of time and store them until you are ready to decorate. If you will be using the cake layers within the next two days, wrap them tightly in foil or plastic wrap and store in a cool place, but not the refrigerator. For longer storage, freeze cakes wrapped in heavy-duty foil or stored in airtight freezer bags. Cakes will keep frozen for up to two months. Thaw frozen cakes, wrapped, at room temperature.

Decorated cakes can also be stored for up to one month. Freeze the unwrapped, frosted cake for 1 to 2 hours or until the frosting has hardened. Then wrap tightly in heavy-duty foil and store in the freezer. Unwrap a decorated cake *before* thawing.

BASE FROSTING

3 cups powdered sugar,
   sifted
½ cup butter or margarine,
   softened
¼ cup milk
½ teaspoon vanilla

Combine powdered sugar, butter, milk and vanilla in large bowl. Beat with electric mixer until smooth. Add more milk, 1 teaspoon at a time. Frosting should be fairly thin.

Makes about 2 cups

JAM GLAZE

1 cup apricot or seedless
   raspberry jam
1 tablespoon water

Bring jam and water to a boil in small saucepan. Remove from heat. Cool before using. Spread over cake and let stand about 1 hour before frosting.

Makes about 1 cup

Note: *Use apricot jam if the cake is being covered by a light frosting. The raspberry jam is particularly good with chocolate cake and frosting.*

UNCOOKED FONDANT

¼ cup butter or margarine,
   softened
4 cups powdered sugar,
   sifted
¼ cup evaporated milk
1 teaspoon vanilla

Beat butter in medium bowl until light and fluffy. Gradually beat in powdered sugar. Beat in milk and vanilla. Knead on surface sprinkled with additional powdered sugar until smooth and glossy. Divide in portions, knead in paste color and shape as desired. Uncooked fondant can be well wrapped and refrigerated overnight or frozen several weeks. Bring to room temperature before using.

Makes about 1 cup

CHOCOLATE BUTTERCREAM FROSTING

6 cups powdered sugar, sifted and divided
1 cup butter or margarine, softened
4 to 6 squares (1 ounce each) unsweetened chocolate, melted and cooled slightly
8 to 10 tablespoons milk, divided
1 teaspoon vanilla

Combine 3 cups powdered sugar, butter, melted chocolate, to taste, 6 tablespoons milk and vanilla in large bowl. Beat with electric mixer until smooth. Add remaining powdered sugar; beat until light and fluffy, adding more milk, 1 tablespoon at a time, as needed for good spreading consistency.

Makes about 3½ cups

BUTTERCREAM FROSTING

6 cups powdered sugar, sifted and divided
¾ cup butter or margarine, softened
¼ cup shortening
6 to 8 tablespoons milk, divided
1 teaspoon vanilla

Combine 3 cups powdered sugar, butter, shortening, 4 tablespoons milk and vanilla in large bowl. Beat with electric mixer until smooth. Add remaining powdered sugar; beat until light and fluffy, adding more milk, 1 tablespoon at a time, as needed for good spreading consistency.

Makes about 3½ cups

LIGHT & FLUFFY FROSTING

2 egg whites*
⅔ cup sugar
5 tablespoons light corn syrup
Dash salt
1 teaspoon vanilla

Combine egg whites, sugar, corn syrup and salt in top of double boiler or stainless steel bowl. Set over boiling water. Beat constantly with electric mixer until stiff peaks form, about 7 minutes. Remove from water and beat in vanilla.

Makes about 2 cups

*Use clean, uncracked eggs

SKILL LEVEL INDEX